Beautiful Flowers
COLOR BY NUMBERS

Beautiful Flowers
COLOR BY NUMBERS

SIRIUS

ISBN: 978-1-3988-4045-4
CH011884NT
Supplier 29, Date 0424, PI 00005890

Printed in China

INTRODUCTION

Whether in a rolling field spotted with bright wildflowers or a lush bouquet, flowers are a delight to everyone. With blooms from throughout the globe and for every style and taste, this color-by-numbers collection will allow you to revel in the vast array of flowers that beautify our world.

Channel your innermost green thumb and design your own special garden from the idyllic images in this book. Each artwork is numbered to the corresponding color key, which you can match to your personal set of colored pencils. If there is no number, the space should be left white or colored with a white pencil.

You may even want to try exploring different shades or styles; the possibilities are endless! Whatever you choose, let your creativity bloom and watch your vibrant garden slowly come to life without getting any dirt on your hands. While the more complex images will require time and patience, it will be hugely rewarding to watch your garden grow.

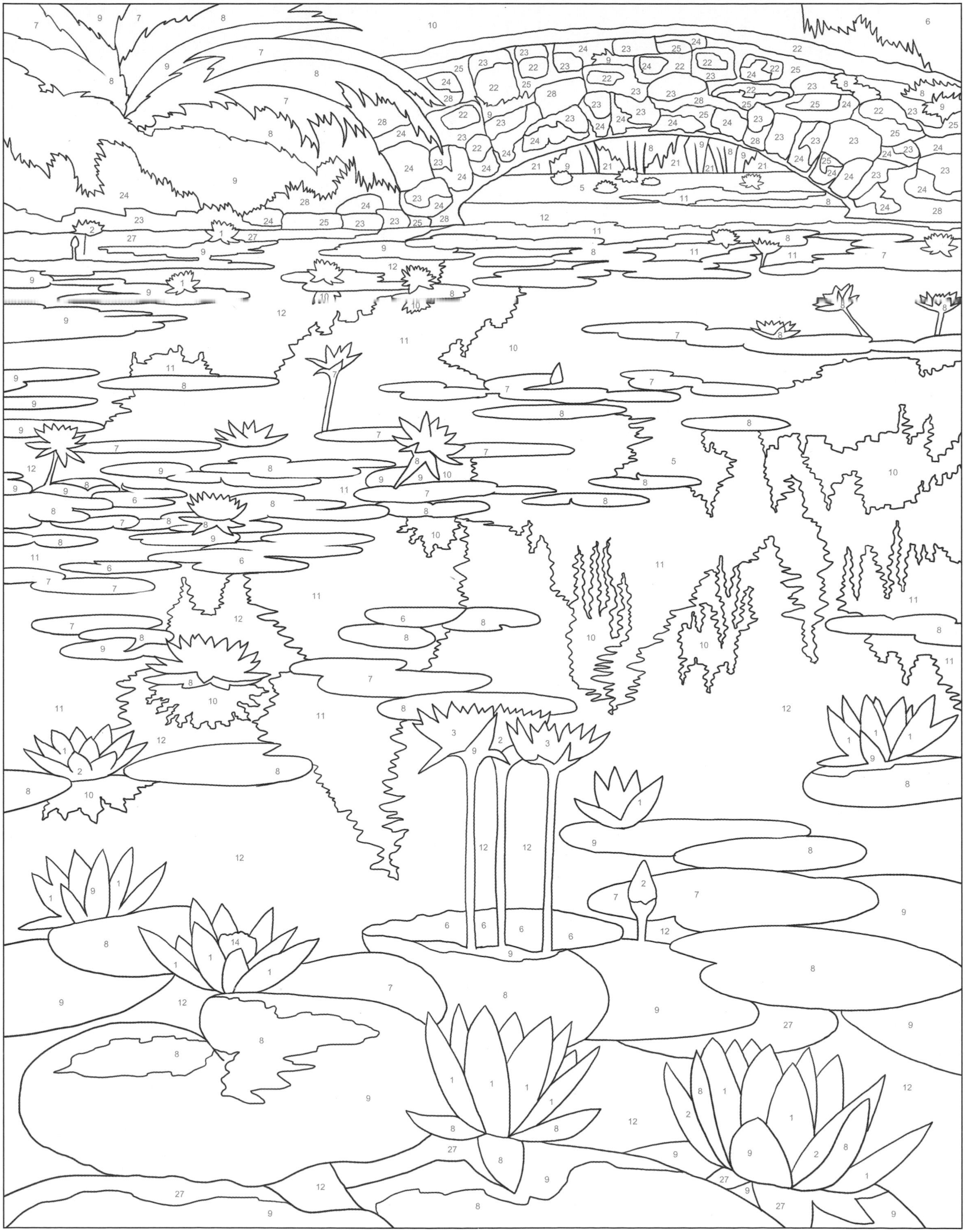